The No-Nonsense Guide to Good Parenting
by Nanny Phillips

Copyright 2018

CW00952200

Disclaimer:

Contents

Introduction

Let's get this out of the way first of all: I'm old-fashioned and I make no apology for being so. I'm also a no-nonsense, rather politically-incorrect sort of person and this is a no-nonsense, rather politically-incorrect sort of book.

If you are looking for some 'progressive' parenting advice that panders to all the politically-correct sensitivities of our modern society, then I'm afraid you're going to have to look elsewhere, because you won't find that sort of nonsense here. I do not think children should have to be wary of committing inadvertent 'micro-aggressions' and I do not think 'gender-fluid parenting' is a remotely sane idea under any circumstances!

This is my perspective: I've been looking after children, privately and professionally, for most of my life - and whilst I'm perfectly aware that there have always been people who are not especially good at being parents, I particularly despair at the sort of parenting standards I often see on display in today's society and I dread to think how bad parenting standards are behind closed doors.

Like me, you've probably seen those parents in the supermarket, their child throwing a tantrum on the supermarket floor or in some other way making a ridiculous fuss over something or other. And what are those parents doing? They're frantically trying to bribe their little brat with promises of sweets or other undeserved treats, in a desperate attempt to calm them down - a strategy that is very obviously going to exacerbate the overall problem. This sort of frankly pathetic, namby-pamby parenting is unfortunately all too common these days.

It's hardly surprising then, that we wind up with our current epidemic of spoilt, ludicrously-sensitive, 'snowflake' college students who throw a temper tantrum whenever a visiting speaker says something they don't want to hear. They expect to be protected from free speech, in case they find it offensive. They appear terrified that hearing an opinion they don't happen to agree with might 'trigger' some sort of allergic reaction. In my view, their parents must have done something terribly wrong to have produced such pathetic, weak-minded offspring.

And many people go on acting like selfish, inconsiderate, spoilt children, even when they're supposed to be full adults and have responsibility for children of their own.

So, yes, I'm very concerned about the state of parenting skills in our modern societies - and I want to try to do my bit to improve the situation.

And in my view, the nonsense of modern political-correctness is not just a symptom of the problem. It is a major *cause* of the problem. I can't abide political-correctness in any case, but it seems to me that parenting is one of those areas of life that has been most seriously harmed by it. I get especially angry and upset when it interferes with and undermines good parenting - and when it encourages the sort of nonsense ideas and nonsense attitudes that do real and lasting damage to children.

Modern political-correctness undermines parents in two main ways. The first is that it constantly disparages traditional parenting methods, whilst rarely advocating any workable, sensible alternatives.

If you discipline children, take away their privileges, or even so much as criticise them or tell them off, the politically-correct zealots of this world are all too eager to denounce you as a bad parent.

New parents are faced with an enormous amount of PC snottiness about what parenting techniques are not appropriate and no longer acceptable. There's so much tut-tutting about what they aren't supposed to do, that many parents are very unsure indeed about what they *are* supposed to do.

Consequently, a lot of parents are actually too afraid to do much parenting at all. They're too embarrassed about possibly getting it wrong and being frowned at, criticised, ridiculed, or even reported to the authorities, that they shy away from active parenting - as if it is better not to bother, than to try hard and be criticised anyway.

Parents stand back and let schools, the TV, the games console, mobile phones, the internet and other children take over the job of parenting - but schools, the TV, the games console, mobile phones, the internet and other children are terrible at parenting. No parent is perfect, but this 'not parenting' strategy is disastrous - much worse than just being moderately inept.

And when today's parents are eventually forced to do some parenting - when their offspring get completely out of hand and have already become spoilt brats - they're often so timid and unsure of themselves that they make the situation worse, rather than better.

What parents usually need is some firm, simple, practical, plainly-spoken parenting advice. Unfortunately, they rarely get it - and once again, this is due to political-correctness.

You see; the second major way in which political-correctness undermines good parenting, is by encouraging people - parents included - to be so ridiculously sensitive to criticism and so quick to take offence, that other people become extremely reluctant to offer them the advice they clearly need.

In today's hyper-sensitive society, almost any advice is automatically interpreted as criticism - and most people seem to have been rigorously brainwashed to take offence over any form of criticism, no matter how kindly it is meant or how helpful it could potentially be.

And when it is parenting advice, the situation is even worse. Simply offering parenting advice to a mother may quickly be interpreted as nothing but a thinly-disguised insult to her parenting skills; just an underhand way of saying, 'You are a terrible mother!' Little or no account is taken of how good the advice is, or how urgently it was required. Offence may simply be taken over the fact that advice was offered at all.

And yet, despite this, there may still be many parents who might actually welcome some no-nonsense parenting advice. Unfortunately, even then, most people are generally just too afraid to offer it. They're too terrified that it might cause offence - and they don't want to take that risk.

Even many grandparents are reluctant to offer advice, for fear that their own over-pampered offspring will ostracise them if they dare to venture an opinion on their parenting skills.

Furthermore, we have this ridiculous, politically-correct mantra, so often repeated, that 'parents know best.' Well, some of them are experienced experts, but most are not. Most of them are badly in need of advice - however much they might be reluctant to admit it.

It is in the hope of helping to tackle these problems, that I have written this book. If you are a parent - or if you are soon to be a parent, or even just hoping to become a parent - and if you're not one of those oversensitive imbeciles who react aggressively to well-intended advice, then you may find this book rather helpful. It can be used as a useful source for the sort of helpful advice that most people nowadays will be either unable to give you, or too reluctant to give you, for reasons of political-correctness.

You can pick up and read a book, and take or leave the advice it contains, as you see fit. I don't know anything about you as a parent - so the advice in this book can hardly be seen as a comment on your parenting skills, or lack thereof, or as personal criticism - so there's no excuse for taking offence.

Unlike most other people, I'm not afraid of being politically-incorrect or of being tutted at for giving 'unacceptable' or 'inappropriate' advice. I reject most politically-correct parenting techniques. I prefer old-fashioned, no-nonsense parenting techniques - not out of sentimental nostalgia, but because they work - and I am in no way reluctant to say so.

This book is intended to be the antithesis of the namby-pamby sort of parenting advice you're most likely to get these days. It is intended to provide no-nonsense, practical and common sense advice that you might struggle to get elsewhere. And if anyone considers it old-fashioned or inappropriate: Tough!

If you are a parent or a prospective parent or are just looking to the future, I hope you find my ideas to be helpful as you face all those important decisions that lie ahead. You're looking forward to a potentially wonderful adventure. I wish you every success in that adventure - and if my advice proves at all helpful to you, then I will be very pleased to have been of some service to you.

Kind Regards, Nanny Phillips

Preparation

The job of being a good parent starts a lot earlier than the moment of birth. It starts a lot earlier than the moment of conception. It starts before you've found yourself a partner - or, as we used to say in the old days, a husband or wife!

Being a good parent requires preparation - whether that comes about through happy accident or by design. You need to build yourself into the sort of person who is going to make a good parent. Your job doesn't have to be finished by the time of the birth - it almost certainly won't be - but it really would help if you had at least laid down some reasonably serviceable foundations by that time.

I'm now going to be blunt with you, because I don't believe in pussyfooting around: To be a good parent, you have to stop being a selfish, overgrown child yourself. And let's face it; that's what an awful lot of today's adults essentially are. They are immature people who have never themselves grown up enough to think much beyond satisfying their own selfish and silly desires. And the trouble is that selfish, immature people do not make good parents. So, most prospective parents need to grow up a little themselves.

Furthermore, if you want your kids to be healthy, happy, confident, well-educated, kind and considerate, then it is really going to help if you are a healthy, happy, confident, well-educated, kind and considerate person yourself.

We've all seen, for example, those unhealthy, overweight kids in the supermarket, and looked at their parents, and been in little doubt where the kids get their unhealthy eating and low exercise habits from. And being a stick insect won't help either, of course.

Ill-health isn't always brought on by unhealthy lifestyles - and having ill-health does not necessarily preclude you from being a fantastic parent.

It is important, however, that you do what you reasonably can to keep yourself healthy - not just so you can be around long enough to be of most use to your children, but so you can set a good example.

How, for example, are you going to get your kids to eat healthily, if you don't eat healthily yourself? It is technically possible that a parent can feed their children healthily, whilst eating junk themselves. In most cases, however, parents who fail to feed themselves healthy food, will also fail when it comes to their children.

The trouble is that even when your own parents bring you up eating healthily throughout your childhood, there often comes a period in your life when healthy eating is far from your top priority.

I expect it was great going out for some serious drinking sessions. It was great tucking into those late-night kebabs on the way home. It was convenient to eat those ready-meals when you were living in student digs or by yourself. You only had one person to feed. It wasn't worth going to too much bother, was it?

Living this way may not do too much harm if you only do so for a short period. The trouble is, however, that it often isn't just a short period anymore. It used to be for just a few years whilst people were at college and/or during the first few years of their working lives - perhaps even into their mid-twenties.

Nowadays, however, it often extends well into their thirties - and by the time they are thinking of settling down and starting a family, their bodies have already been ravaged by perhaps fifteen years or so of unhealthy living.

It just isn't a very good start when new parents are already rather unhealthy - perhaps even somewhat blimp-like. Unhealthy parents are all too likely to bring up unhealthy children.

And there are many other vices to consider, besides eating unhealthily; smoking, excessive drinking, lack of exercise.

Now I'm not here to judge you or your bad habits - but I am here to tell you that such habits do not fit well with being a good parent. An occasional indulgence is one thing - but when they become habitual, that's a problem.

So, whatever unhealthy excesses you might be used to or might have enjoyed in the past, it is time to let them go when you decide to try to become a parent.

But preparation is about much more than healthy living. Yes, if you don't live a healthy lifestyle, your children probably won't do either, but also; if you are not well-educated, your children probably won't be well-educated either.

As parents, you will be the directors of your child's education. It will be your job to check that they are receiving the education they deserve. If they are let down by their teachers, for example, you ought to be able to recognise and help rectify the problem.

You don't have to be an expert in every educational area, as you will probably not be educating your child by yourself, but if you are not a reasonably well-educated person, it may be very difficult to competently fulfil your role of being your child's educational overseer.

And there are all sorts of practical skills you can helpfully develop. Can you cook? Can you swim?

Can you play chess? Can you fix a bike or a computer? The sooner you can pick these skills up, the better.

But even if you *are* ready to be a good parent, what about your partner?

And the first step towards getting them ready for parenthood, is to pick the right person in the first place - someone with the right attitudes and values to enable them to become a successful parent too.

And yet, picking a partner on a rational basis of whether they will make a good mother or good father, might seem somewhat out of place with modern attitudes.

Many people seem to have this idea that you should just fall in love, and that the falling in love has nothing to do with (and, perhaps, that it *should* have nothing to do with) making a rational assessment of that person's character and abilities and, most importantly of all, their potential as a prospective parent. The modern attitude seems to be that there is something almost sordid about making rational assessments in matters of relationships.

To some extent, instinct and rationality have worked hand in hand over the centuries. We are naturally attracted to features and characteristics that tend towards making a person a good parent and a good husband or wife - but modern fashions and norms sometimes differ from the traditional ones and the ones that are rightly associated with suitability for parenthood.

For example, when it comes to relationships, society seems almost to applaud people for selfishness. 'Can my partner give me what I want?' we are encouraged to ask. It is hardly any wonder, then, that so many relationships and marriages end up in acrimony and divorce. Selfishness is no basis for a successful relationship.

No, if you want a successful long-term relationship, the thing at the very top of your list should be your potential partner's suitability as a parent. Unless you don't want children at all, there can be nothing more important to the long-term health of your relationship than whether your partner has the potential to be a great parent.

Attitude

Being a good parent isn't just about skills and experience. It's about attitudes, too. And before we go any further, I want to address the subject of one particular sort of bad attitude that seems to be extremely common in our societies today. It's an issue about the stages of life and how modern society encourages us to view them.

As we all know, there's a period in many people's late teens or early twenties when a person is expected to enjoy the indulgences of youth. Perhaps they are attending university or perhaps they are in employment, but they haven't yet got a family to support or a mortgage to keep up with. So, much of their money and time is theirs to do with as they wish. They have relatively few responsibilities or commitments. Very often, they get to spend their money on themselves and on having (or on trying to have) a good time. These are, essentially, the drinking years. You get to stay up late, go to parties, drink lots of alcohol and generally please yourself.

Now, I'm not saying that there is anything wrong with indulging yourself somewhat at this stage of life. You might not believe it now, but I was quite a raver myself, once upon a time! And yes, it is great, in many ways, to be young and relatively carefree, if you can manage it.

Now, however, there seems to be a prevalent and very misleading social attitude that causes people to believe that these drinking years are the best years of your life - an attitude that leads to people desperately trying to extend these drinking years for as long as possible, as if life will never be this good again.

In times not so long ago, people used to indulge

in this way for three or four years, or perhaps even five or six - but it wouldn't be too long before they were mentally ready to move on to new and better things. Specifically, their thoughts would turn to 'settling down' to experience the joys of starting and raising a family.

But modern society's obsession with youth and with the drinking culture encourages people to take the attitude that these drinking years should be extended into your thirties or even forties - and even that, ideally, they should never end. It's an attitude that says that going out with mates and getting drunk is the best thing that can ever happen in life, so you should want to do as much of it as possible and as little as possible of anything else.

Well, let me tell you something: It isn't the best thing in life. In fact, it doesn't come anywhere even close to the wonders of having and raising children.

And the really big problem here, is not so much that people are extending their drinking years and leaving it ever later to start a family - with possible infertility issues and other problems that this may lead to. The biggest problem may be that, even when people do 'settle down' and start a family, instead of enjoying this new stage of life and really enjoying the wonders of family life, they instead get stuck in hankering after the past.

Instead of enjoying being a parent, they're always looking over their shoulders at those drinking years. They're missing the joys of parenthood, because they've been conditioned to believe that the best years of their lives are already behind them and that the best they can hope for is to recreate that lifestyle at any opportunity.

Being a good parent, however, *is* indeed the best thing in life - but you'll struggle to be a good parent if, instead of enjoying being a parent, you spend time resenting being a parent and resenting the responsibilities that go with it.

Well, wake up! Those responsibilities are great. They're wonderful. They're enjoyable. Being a good parent to happy and healthy children is simply the best thing ever. It's great fun - and if you can't wake your brain up to realise that, then you really are making parenthood and life in general unnecessarily difficult for yourself.

If you think that being a drunken youth is better or more fun than being a good parent, then you are, I'm sorry to have to say, an idiot - an idiot who has probably been brainwashed by prevailing social attitudes into believing something that is utter nonsense.

Unfortunately, many people develop a bad attitude, under which they seem to feel that parenting gets in the way of their lives, rather than realising that parenting is supposed to be the central part of their lives - and enjoying it as such.

The main thing that might prevent you from having enormous fun being a parent, is an irrational, socially-indoctrinated attitude that prevents you from having fun with your kids. Let go of the past and let yourself be free to enjoy what you are.

The joys of drinking and partying and being care-free; these are nothing compared to the joys of holding your baby and nothing compared to the joys of seeing your kids running around, having fun and growing up to be strong, intelligent and kind. Parenting will be so much more rewarding if you take the time to appreciate this simple fact.

Babies

Looking after a baby can be difficult in a number of ways. It can certainly be tiring. And when they are so small and helpless by themselves, it is difficult not to worry about them. It is, nevertheless, an essentially quite simple task, in most cases.

Babies need to be fed and they need to sleep. They need their nappies changing and they need to be washed. They need stimulation and they need lots and lots of hugs and cuddles. There's really not much more to it than that.

If, as a parent, you can focus on those simple needs - alongside enjoying the fun and privilege of spending time with your little darling - then you should be just fine.

The chief difficulty that arises is not knowing what the baby needs at any particular moment. When babies cry, new parents can sometimes become rather anxious, not knowing exactly why the baby is crying. Are they hungry again? Are they in pain or discomfort? Do they need their nappy changing? Do they need a hug? Are they simply 'over-tired' - i.e. basically just grumpy because they need to sleep?

There is, however, a simple solution: Check their nappy. Change it if it needs changing. Check they're not too hot or too cold. Hug them and walk around for a bit. And if they still cry, then stick them on the boob. If they're hungry, they'll feed. If they're tired, they'll probably feed for a bit and then fall asleep.

If they still cry, then, provided they don't have a temperature or any signs of real illness, they are probably just over-tired. They can simply be put down in their cot, allowed to have a little cry for ten minutes or so - and then they'll be off to sleep.

This is where new parents today need the sort of simple, clear advice that today's political-correctness often denies them: There is absolutely nothing whatsoever wrong with leaving your child to cry in its cot for ten or twenty minutes to get itself off to sleep. You're far more likely to do harm by fretting and going in to pick them up every two minutes, than by letting them cry themselves to sleep. Your over-anxiousness may well be picked up by your child.

It used to be standard advice given to almost all parents - by helpful grandparents, aunts and uncles, for example - not to rush to soothe your baby every time they whimper or make a fuss over something. If you ignore this advice, you will be 'making a rod for your own back,' you would be told.

Very often, unfortunately, parents today either ignore this advice, or it is never given in the first place, thanks to people being fearful that advice will be all too readily interpreted as criticism. This doesn't, however, mean that it isn't still excellent advice, if you are lucky enough to receive it.

So, try hard not be be anxious. That can sound easier than it actually is, so I'll share with you a little secret that might help you enormously. It is not some sort of special nannying secret. It is actually something that is probably known to all competent, experienced parents, but which many new parents don't seems to be aware of, and it is this:

Babies and young toddlers have (at least) two very distinct types of crying. One is of genuine need or distress or discomfort. The other one is a nagging grasp for attention. Experienced, observant parents, so long as they are not over-anxious, can easily pick up the difference between the two.

And as an experienced parent, you often see other parents frequently getting it wrong. You see them fussing over their child and you're thinking; 'That's not a distressed cry. That's just a nagging cry. Can you really not tell the difference?'

I sometimes suspect that pretty much everyone in the world can tell the difference. The only people who can't tell the difference are the child's own over-anxious parents, who are terrified their precious little darlings will never forgive them if they don't instantly attend to their every whim.

So; meet all your child's needs, but don't fret at the mere fact that babies cry quite a lot. Yes, lots of them do. In itself, it's nothing to worry about. It's just their way of trying to communicate. Sure, you may not instantly know what that cry means, but it is almost certainly one of only a few possibilities - so that shouldn't present any real difficulties.

And there are a few other issues I'd like to briefly mention at this point. One of these is the issue of dummies - or 'pacifiers' as my American friends call them. When a baby cries, it can seem like a tempting solution to try to mollify them with a dummy. However, the advice I would give any parent on this issue is very simple advice: Never give a baby a dummy. Never give any child, of any age, a dummy. Just never, ever!

Babies don't want dummies anyway. They want nipples. They want Mummy's snuggly boobies! And if you give them a dummy, you're setting yourself up for a great deal of unnecessary aggro - and you're setting your child up for ongoing problems, that might even last into adulthood, as dummies may well be linked to smoking and obesity in later life.

And if you get a child used to having a dummy, you'll have the whole problem of trying to wean them off the dummy later on - and the possible tantrums that that may well provoke, besides all the dental problems you might cause. But if they're not used to having anything in their mouths, other than when they are hungry, they won't miss having anything in their mouths.

Seriously, the temporary quiet you might get if you give a child a dummy, just isn't worth all the problems it can cause later on.

Another issue you might face at this point is the one about whether you should try to get your baby used to a routine. And the advice I would give is again fairly simple: No. With young babies, you should just feed them when they want feeding, let them sleep when they are tired and let them play when they want to play.

Later on, routine is marvellous. Kids love it. They like to learn how things are organised and can look forward to things which they know are coming up. But for babies; don't worry about it! You just have to arrange your time around their needs, as much as you can.

And finally: Nappies. As I like to say: 'Let it fill, but don't let it linger.' Jump on it too early and they'll just finish off five minutes later in a new nappy. So, keep them clean, but don't rush things.

Breastfeeding

Now we need to address the issue of breastfeeding. There's no getting away from the fact that breastfeeding is wonderful. It has to be right up there as one of the greatest inventions in the universe. Not only does it provide your baby with fantastic nutrition, custom-built for their specific needs, it often also sends them to sleep and may well provide them with levels of security and comfort that nothing else can come close to.

Is it possible to be a good parent without breastfeeding your child? Yes it is, but the fact remains that breastfeeding is almost always the best thing for your child - especially for their first six months or so - and that breastfeeding has huge advantages over bottle-feeding. Not breastfeeding puts your child at a significant disadvantage - and can potentially have negative repercussions for their entire lives.

We know that breastfeeding is wonderful. The trouble is that modern society is rife with practices and attitudes that discourage breastfeeding and can make it difficult or awkward to breastfeed.

In practical terms, one of the biggest problems is obviously the fact that many mothers go out to work. Women who do go back to work obviously can't usually breastfeed their baby whenever it needs feeding - unless they take their baby with them to their place of work. They may express milk, but not being with their baby all the time obviously makes breastfeeding more difficult - and we can see and understand how many of them think that bottle-feeding then becomes a more practical alternative to breastfeeding.

For some women, however, the pressure not to breastfeed doesn't come from such practical considerations. It stems from some frankly obscene social attitudes that are totally at odds with basic good sense.

The look of disgust some people display on their faces when they see a mother breastfeeding in public - well, it just beggars belief that anyone could be so offended over such an innocent and wonderful thing.

Let's not over-dramatise the issue. A bottle-fed baby can, of course, grow up strong and healthy. However, it is a terrible shame that many people forego the advantages of breastfeeding, largely as a result of some ridiculous social attitudes that cause them to feel awkward or embarrassed about breastfeeding.

If, for whatever reason, you decide not to breastfeed - or to cut breastfeeding short - at the very least, don't let it be because you have caved in to social pressure based on our societies' ludicrous anti-breastfeeding prejudices.

If you give in to such pressures, then, frankly, you are failing a basic requirement of good parenting - in that you are failing to put the interests of your child above the ludicrous prejudices of the insane idiots who frown and tut-tut at public breastfeeding.

A good mother whips her boobs out whenever they are needed. It is ridiculous to hold back or find alternative arrangements out of embarrassment. What could you possibly have to be embarrassed about? You're performing one of the most natural and beneficial acts it is possible to perform.

And let's cut out this nonsense suggestion that you should be 'discreet' about it. People who are repulsed by the sight of a mother breastfeeding are.... well, frankly, there's something terribly wrong with them.

If you find that you suffer from this malady, then the thing to do is to realise that you've been conditioned to react in this way. It is something you ought to overcome - because it is an entirely unhelpful, unnatural, unhealthy and damaging reaction. What good can it possibly do you or anyone else? None, is the answer - so get over it!

So, please ladies, when you do breastfeed in public, don't do it in a sheepish, embarrassed fashion, nervously using blankets or other items to cover up every last piece of flesh you can, for fear of offending anyone. If you do that, you're adding to the social stigma problem by encouraging people to see public breastfeeding as something to be ashamed of.

Just whip those boobs out and be completely uninhibited about it and you'll be doing your bit to encourage those mothers who don't have as much confidence as you have. And if anyone has a problem with that, they'll just have to get over it!

Back to Work

Not every mother, unfortunately, has the freedom to stay at home and be a full-time mother. Some have to work. And some choose to work - and I have looked after the children of many perfectly good mothers who have chosen to return to work, even though they didn't really need to.

Nevertheless, if you can devote yourself full-time to being a parent, then that is a wonderful thing to be able to do. Unfortunately, our modern societies often appear to look down upon stay-at-home mothers as if they are second-class citizens in some way.

Well, let's chuck this nonsense out! Mothers who devote themselves above all things to being mothers, are the most wonderful people in the world. And anyone who seeks (or speaks or acts) to denigrate full-time mothers should be ashamed of themselves.

A 'successful woman' should not mean a rich executive. The most successful women of all are successful because they are good mothers.

So, when is it OK for a mother to return to work full-time, after having had a baby? Well, my view is simply this: It is an immensely valuable thing to be able to be with your child full-time, in the first few months of their lives and preferably for the first few years, to form the strongest possible bond - and thus to set them up with the best possible start in life. It is not an opportunity that should be passed up without at least considering it very carefully.

It may be politically-correct to say - and vehemently affirm - that a mother can return quickly to her full-time career, without this having any adverse effect whatsoever on her child, but take a step back and we'll see that this is probably just wishful thinking.

It is the politically-correct position to champion the career woman - and, in itself, that's just fine, but we shouldn't let that position make us blind to obvious realities. In real life, career women do have to make compromises. And, in real life, a baby's well-being is easily compromised by having a mother who returns to work too soon after giving birth.

For one reason or another, however, many mothers do decide to return to work just weeks after giving birth, even when they have the right to remain on paid maternity leave for much longer.

Some fear that their careers will be seriously harmed if they are away from work for too long - and that others will get promotions ahead of them. In some cases, they may be being somewhat paranoid. In other cases, sadly, their suspicions may be correct.

Some women have extremely important work that cannot very easily be done as well by anyone else. Some women genuinely like their jobs and/or the people they work with and don't want to be away from work for more than a few weeks. Others may not particularly like their jobs, but they can't stand the idea of 'hanging around' at home all day.

However, the decision about whether or not to take extended maternity leave (and also whether the father takes advantage of paternity leave) is a hugely important one.

So, if you do return to work early, please make sure it is for good reasons and not because you're essentially being bullied into it, or because you've deceived yourself into believing that mother-baby time isn't so important after all.

There are very significant costs and disadvantages to our modern lifestyles. It has become the norm that both of a child's parents work - often full-time. As a child grows up, the time they get to spend with their parents is often severely limited.

And perhaps worse than that, due to their work commitments and busy lifestyles, parents are often too tired, when they are at home, to properly engage with their children - and often leave the TV, the internet and the games console to babysit their children for them.

This sort of thing can be a huge problem throughout childhood - and it often starts with mothers going back to work too soon after giving birth.

The time you can spend with your child is extremely important. Please don't sacrifice it lightly!

Discipline

Well here I am, talking about discipline already, when we've only just been talking about babies. It is very important that I do so, however, because failure to implement an effective disciplinary system can lead to all manner of serious and long-lasting behavioural problems that you should be extremely keen to avoid.

Discipline is every bit as much a part of loving your child as are hugs or bedtime stories. Unfortunately, thanks to nonsensical political-correctness, 'discipline' is often regarded as a dirty word these days - but it shouldn't be.

As a society, so many of the problems we face (from crime to the obesity crisis) are caused by adults with behavioural problems - behavioural problems that could and should have been dealt with when they were children. Unfortunately, their parents often failed to implement a clear and consistent disciplinary system. And without discipline, many millions of children have grown up to be selfish, greedy, inconsiderate adults.

I suspect even our economic problems are often ultimately due to inadequate parenting. I can't help but think that if I could have taken some of today's unethical, greedy and dishonest corporate executives and put them over my knee when they were young, they would never have turned out so badly - and we wouldn't have half the problems we have now.

Parents have a duty to deal with children's behavioural problems, so that those children won't then grow up to be the inconsiderate, greedy, selfish adults that blight our societies. The fundamental cause of so many of our problems is that far too many of today's adults just weren't brought up properly.

So, how do you construct a good disciplinary system?

Well, firstly, any prospective parent should take some time to consider and appreciate the basic principles of good discipline, so that they can be confident in their approach and not get easily blown off course by the demands or criticisms of modern political-correctness.

Using a 'first principles' sort of approach, we know that it is necessary to exert a certain amount of control over children. We have to stop them running into the road, touching hot pans on the stove or hitting other children. And we should be prepared to use physical restraint if necessary. There are many things that children have a tendency to do or to try to do, but which we, as responsible adults, do not allow them to do - sometimes because it is dangerous and sometimes because it is wrong.

However, even as parents, we can't always be physically on hand for our children, especially as they get older. So, it becomes our job, as parents, to help our children develop good habits of behaviour, so that they can learn to make good behavioural choices for themselves, even when we are not around.

Children sometimes need to be convinced not to engage in dangerous, harmful or mean behaviour - and they may sometimes need some encouragement to be good. Sometimes, quite understandably, children do not always properly consider the consequences of their actions and may have to be coached to be more considerate.

Now, as children mature, there will, hopefully, come a stage when all issues can simply be discussed and considered - logically and reasonably. The philosophical rights and wrongs can be analysed at length and the child will be mature enough to be able to see the sense of certain rules and will be sufficiently mature to stick to those rules. But what do we do in the meantime, before that day arrives?

Well, there is, of course, a tried and tested solution that has been in use for thousands of years; a measured, consistent and coherent system of punishments and rewards. And such a solution is just as relevant today as it has ever been - regardless of how much many politically-correct zealots might try to claim otherwise!

As a parent, you simply use rewards to encourage good behaviour and punishments to discourage poor behaviour. A child who behaves well may get treats and privileges. A child who misbehaves can be punished.

Punishments are not difficult to devise. Toys and games can be taken away. Television time, phone time, tablet time and computer time can be taken away. Games consoles can be put away in the cupboard. Children can be made to stand in the corner or to go to bed early. They can write lines. They can do extra chores. In short; the things they like can be taken away, and they can be made to do things they dislike doing. Simple as that!

Punishments do not need to be cruel or harsh. The essential thing is to be absolutely firm in your approach.

Your job is to make sure that good behaviour is appreciated and rewarded and that bad behaviour not only never pays, but always results in consequences that the child would wish to avoid.

But if it is really so simple, why do so many parents fail to implement any sort of coherent disciplinary system for their children? Why do so many parents stand idly by as their kids go off the rails?

Well, there are a number of interrelated reasons why such failures occur. For one thing, many parents become unsure and hesitant in the face of the ludicrous demands of political-correctness. They're afraid they'll be looked down upon and criticised - or even reported - if they 'discipline' their children.

Really, there is nothing wrong with the idea of disciplining a child and nothing wrong with punishing a naughty child. It is, after all, in children's own interests that they don't grow up to be selfish, inconsiderate louts. Discipline - sometimes including punishment - is entirely in their interests, as well as in yours.

Discipline mainly just means setting boundaries on what is and is not allowed, and encouraging children to make good decisions about their own behaviour. What could possibly be wrong with that? Of course, there is nothing fundamentally wrong with that at all.

We have a duty to protect children and prevent them doing things that are dangerous or damaging or grossly unhealthy. Just as we must stop them playing on railway tracks, we must protect their health by preventing them from gorging on sweets, fizzy drinks and junk food. And just as we must protect them from being harmed by others, we must prevent them from harming others.

So, we exert control to limit their behaviour in childhood. We also hope and intend that discipline in their childhood will have positive effects on how they behave as adults. And there's nothing immoral about that! Of course, when they are grown up, they will become responsible for their own behaviour, but we still have a duty to set them off in the right direction.

"But couldn't we 'discipline' children and encourage good behaviour without punishing them?" some may ask.

Well, many 'punishments' are not really punishments in the traditional sense of the word. Banning a child from using their games console, for example, is not really a punishment. Having a games console is a privilege, not a right - and it is a privilege that should be reserved for well-behaved children. Withdrawal of a privilege is a little different from an out-and-out punishment.

And in the modern age, children have so many toys and games and privileges, that taking such things away is usually a very effective 'punishment.' They are so used to having their games and toys and luxuries, that the sanction of having them taken away, even for a short time, is usually sufficient to get them to make an effort to significantly improve their behaviour.

But real punishments can be used, too. The traditional 'standing in the corner' punishment works extremely well for young children. It doesn't suddenly or magically become ineffective just because it may no longer be considered politically-correct.

Some people have tried to use systems that only use rewards, never punishments - but they often seem to involve children being rewarded simply because they were not quite so badly behaved as usual. And when children get rewarded, even though they have behaved badly, that's obviously sending completely the wrong message - so it's no wonder such approaches usually end up in abject failure.

And there's no good reason why we should be striving to avoid using punishments anyway. Stupid behaviour often has quite severe natural consequences. If you run into the road without looking or play with electrical sockets, you can get yourself killed. If you fail to eat healthily, you can knock decades off your lifespan. If you start fights, you may get punched in the face. If you are selfish and inconsiderate, you may be in for a lifetime of misery.

But with children, we try to protect them from the natural consequences of their often unwise behaviour. We still want them to learn from their mistakes, however, so we replace natural consequences with far less severe, artificial consequences, which still enable the child to learn their lesson, but without permanent damage.

The PC assumption that punishments are harmful is completely wrong. Reasonable punishments aren't harming your child. They are protecting your child - both when they are young and when they become adults.

Doing dangerous things leads to real harm. Starting fights leads to real harm. Being selfish and inconsiderate leads to real harm. But making a child stand in the corner for ten minutes causes them no harm whatsoever. Banning a child from the games console for a day or a week causes no harm whatsoever. Raising your voice to a child who has been naughty causes no harm whatsoever. A mild slap on the leg of a naughty child causes no harm whatsoever.

Others will disagree with me - but where is their evidence? On the other hand, there is a vast amount of evidence that not disciplining a child can have extremely damaging consequences. It's not like in the old days, when children used to get the cane. Punishments today are generally very mild in nature - and nothing really to be complaining about!

Part of the problem here is the modern namby-pamby nonsense that encourages people to believe that children are incredibly delicate and that even raising your voice to a child could cause serious and long-lasting damage to their mental well-being.

Many people are so taken in by such unscientific, politically-correct hogwash, that they come to believe that even mildly punishing a child when they are naughty is pretty much akin to child abuse or that simply telling them off is a form of violence. What utter nonsense!

There's even a common and incredibly ridiculous belief that merely criticising a child can 'make them insecure for life.' What really makes a child insecure, of course, is if you artificially shield them from criticism, such that they never learn to cope with it in a mature and sensible way.

Children who are used to honest criticism won't have a problem with it. It is the ones who have been ridiculously mollycoddled that will be the ones who can't cope with it. That's how we've ended up with these snowflake college students who can't cope with criticism and disagreement in a grown-up fashion and who throw temper tantrums when they don't get their way over something or simply because someone else refuses to agree with their harebrained beliefs and opinions.

Of course, caving in to the demands of political-correctness isn't the only reason why parents fail to discipline their child.

Some parents, for example, quickly take the

attitude that firm discipline doesn't work. Well; it does! If there is a problem, it is usually because the parents have been too weak, too easily-manipulated and too lazy to get the job done properly and consistently.

Children are very rarely completely stupid. They quickly realise when poor behaviour is not getting them what they want. They quickly realise when poor behaviour attracts punishments or loss of privileges. They will soon get the idea that bad behaviour attracts unpleasant consequences - so long as you are firm and totally consistent with them.

Unfortunately, a great many parents aren't so bright and they often allow themselves to be manipulated by their children into giving undeserved treats - or even actually rewarding poor behaviour.

Sometimes, parents are overly soft because they are pursuing a misguided strategy to try to give themselves a quiet time. They don't want trouble. They don't want an argument. So, they give in and allow poor behaviour to go unchecked. Fairly obviously, this soon leads to far more trouble than they would have had to deal with if they had simply taken a firm line in the first place and cracked down on poor behaviour the moment it started. Be consistent and firm. There is no better strategy for an easy life than that.

There is a very reasonable view that parents should try to explain things to children and point out why something is wrong, instead of simply punishing children for poor behaviour, as if that is the only thing they will respond to. And I agree with this view. Parents should talk to their children and discuss issues of manners, consideration and ethical behaviour.

In practice, however, a sensible discussion isn't always going to be enough to get the job done efficiently all by itself. Sensible words will often need to be accompanied by fair, but firm punishments, to get the message through.

Next we have the problem of false friendships. This is where parents fail to discipline children because, instead of doing their jobs as parents, they are just so incredibly desperate to be their child's 'friend.' They act as if they are terrified that if they tell their child off or take some toys away for a bit, the child won't then be their friend anymore. It's a ridiculous, very childish concern, but many parents still have it nevertheless.

But here's the thing: In being a good parent - and sometimes a strict one - you *are* being a good friend. But you are being a true friend, not the sort of please-like-me, clingy sort of friend that is so much more common these days.

Needing to be that sort of friend just makes you a selfish person. You're not being a friend to your child that way. You're being a burden to them. By needing their approval, you need them to make you feel good about yourself. That's taking, not giving!

No. Children need discipline. And if they behave badly, parents should not feel ashamed to use punishments, nor reluctant to apply them when they are required in the interests of discouraging poor behaviour.

Next, it would be somewhat remiss of me not to tackle head-on the very controversial subject of smacking.

So, what about smacking? Well, smacking is something I wouldn't usually recommend or encourage - for reasons I will explain in due course.

I don't, however, hold with all this PC tosh that assumes that even the mildest of disciplinary smacks is necessarily a form of child abuse. I regard such claims as hysterical nonsense.

Whilst it is perfectly reasonable to wish to avoid smacking a child, lots of loving and perfectly reasonable parents use an occasional mild smack to help keep their over-excitable children from getting too big for their boots - and they do so without causing their child any harm whatsoever.

Are there better ways to discipline children? Often, yes - but not necessarily always.

Suppose, for example, that you have a child who kicks up a big fuss and refuses to eat the healthy meal that you have made for them. If you do not insist they eat the food they have been given, then the consequences can be cruel and long-lasting. They may then be tempted to make a fuss at every meal time. They may avoid healthy food, their health may suffer and they may carry on eating unhealthily throughout their adult life. Your failure to insist that they eat the healthy food you give them could knock many years off their lives. Hopefully, we can agree that that is not an option for a decent, caring parent.

So, what do you do? You could insist that the child sits in their chair, with nothing to play with and nothing to do, until they eat the food they have been given. It hardly seems reasonable, however, to condemn a parent who decides that it is far better and far less cruel to apply a quick smack and get the whole issue settled in a matter of seconds, rather than have it dragged out for hours, possibly with the child screaming and crying most of the time.

Decent, loving parents sometimes consider a mild

smack to be in the best interests of their child, because it is the most practical measure available to them in a given circumstance. And it seems unreasonable to jump to the conclusion that they must necessarily be wrong about that.

'But doesn't smacking teach children that violence is the way to solve their problems?' some people may ask. Well, no - no it doesn't! What it teaches them is that poor behaviour has consequences.

If it also teaches them that force can be used to solve some problems, then that's fine, because force can indeed be used to solve some problems. Very few people actually believe that all use of force is unethical. We support the imprisonment of violent criminals. And we support the idea that we should be prepared to use force to defend ourselves from foreign invaders. But there are times when force is justified and times when it is not.

There's a very big difference between using reasonable, measured and justifiable force in a good cause and using excessive, unjustified force in a bad cause. And it is a silly idea that children somehow aren't capable of telling the difference between force used out of spite and malice and force used as part of a perfectly fair and reasonable disciplinary system. Children aren't generally anywhere near as stupid as many people seem to want to make out.

To say that it may be preferable to try to reason with a child - that's fine! But that's not the same as being able to convincingly argue that the use of any physical chastisement is always wrong or that it can never play a positive role and never be in the interests of any child.

Having said all this, however, I wouldn't, as I say,

actually want to encourage physical chastisement.

This is not, however, because it is inherently wrong - as I don't think it is. Rather, it is because some people are not all that good at controlling their tempers and they might end up smacking a child, not as a measured and carefully considered part of a fair and reasonable disciplinary system, but when they, the parents, have had a hard day at work, are tired or frustrated for other reasons or when they have drunk too much. And parents who are liable to such tendencies might indeed be better off having a rule that they don't smack their children at all.

So I would actually say to parents: Don't smack children, unless you can be extremely confident that you would only resort to physical chastisement when it is entirely reasonable to do so.

And when all is said and done, firm discipline isn't about imposing harsh punishments. It is about being consistent and about using a logical system of escalation in order to provide children with the necessary incentives to improve their behaviour.

Let me explain what I mean: What a lot of parents get wrong is that they fail to appreciate that it is no good telling a child to stop misbehaving and then, if they ignore you, simply telling them the same thing again. If you do that, there is no proper incentive for them to listen to you in the first place.

Tell them to behave themselves - and if they do not instantly improve their behaviour, you should start applying disciplinary measures without delay. It doesn't have to be anything particularly harsh. Make them stand in the corner for two minutes, perhaps! But what you must not do is simply tell them the same thing again without applying any punishments.

What should be obvious is that if you only apply actual punishments after you have told them off three times, then you are essentially training them to think they are allowed to ignore you the first two times you tell them to behave themselves.

If you have to tell a child off twice before they improve their behaviour, they should get punished for poor behaviour *and* punished for ignoring you in the first place. They should accumulate punishments every time they fail to take an opportunity to improve their behaviour. That way, they'll quickly learn to listen to your instructions the first time around! It's basically that simple in the vast majority of cases.

It's a very effective system that I like to call, 'The Accumulator,' because the child accumulates punishments every time they fail to take an opportunity to improve their behaviour. Incentives are important and The Accumulator gives children the incentives they need.

That's how you get well-behaved children! Be determined and consistent. Never back down in the face of bad behaviour. And make sure that it is never worthwhile for your child to persist with bad behaviour.

Toddlers

Very often, the first really serious disciplinary issues occur when children go through their 'terrible twos.' And, in some ways, this may be the most crucial time in a child's upbringing, because if you fail to properly and decisively deal with the behavioural problems you may well experience at this time, it is entirely possible that your child may never fully recover from your parenting failure at this crucial stage of their life.

This is not to say that such failures cannot be recovered from, but recovering from them later is likely to be exponentially harder than dealing effectively with behavioural problems in the first place, before any really serious behavioural problems fully develop.

The 'terrible twos' is a phase of stroppy, sometimes extremely disruptive behaviour that many children go through around the time of their third year in life. The child in question will often attempt to assert their will in an aggressive manner and by exhibiting very poor behaviour, likely to include such behaviours as temper tantrums, screaming fits, extreme lack of cooperation and possibly even hitting and biting.

The basic strategy employed by children going through this phase is essentially to do whatever they can to make life unpleasant for other people, until those other people get fed up and give in to their demands.

Now, not all children go through these 'terrible twos' - and for some children, with good parenting, it takes all of five minutes for them to realise that a temper tantrum is obviously not going to work - and they never try it again.

But, with poor parenting, the terrible twos can

last, not just for years, not just throughout childhood, but into adulthood too!

We end up with adults, who, although they no longer literally kick and scream about on the supermarket floor, still maintain a terrible twos attitude. In other words; when faced with a situation they don't like, they still adopt the general strategy of throwing a temper tantrum in some way - and generally being stroppy and causing trouble - until the people around them give in to their demands.

It is a strategy which, although it sometimes appears to work, in that it gets them what they demand, is only likely to lead to a lifetime of failed relationships. These are the people whose personal relationships consistently fail, because they view the people around them as people to exploit and never manage to develop any truly deep, caring and meaningful relationships.

They end up with a great deal of general misery that they could have easily avoided if only they had ever learnt to deal with problems and disagreements in a more mature, mutually-beneficial manner.

The best way to deal with the terrible twos, is to be ready for them. When your child first tries it on, by throwing a tantrum or refusing to cooperate, you should be ready to meet their stroppiness with total intransigence and complete determination that they will and must lose any battle of wills that ensues at this point.

You come down on them, as we used to say, 'like a ton of bricks.' You are ready to make it 100% clear to your child that tantrums or other stroppy behaviour will get them exactly the opposite of whatever it is they actually want.

Not only do they not get the new toy they are

demanding; they get their existing toys taken away and locked in a cupboard. Not only do they not get to stay up late; they get to go to bed early and have their cuddly toys taken away.

If, on this first occasion when they throw a big strop, they lose out 'big time,' they may never even bother ever trying the tactic again.

As I said in the last chapter; when children behave badly, it is your job, as a parent, not only to make sure that their bad behaviour doesn't get them what they want - as that would obviously encourage bad behaviour - but also to make sure they lose out very substantially as a result of their poor behaviour.

They don't just not get what they want. They get precisely what they don't want. Standing in the corner, toys or treats taken away - there are many options which have proven successful over the centuries. But whatever option you use, temper tantrums must never be allowed to work.

It is a simple matter of incentives and consistency. If you are consistent from the start, this phase of bad behaviour will almost certainly be short-lived. Your child will very quickly realise that temper tantrum tactics aren't going to work.

Be ultra-prepared for this critical moment in your child's life. If you falter at this crucial point, you and your child may pay a heavy price for your weakness.

"You want a new toy, do you Johnny? Well, new toys are only for good children. And bad children not only don't get new toys; bad children get to have all of their nice toys taken away. Treats are only for good children. Naughty children get things taken away."

It is, essentially, that simple. You just need to stick to your guns - rigorously and without exception. A moment of weakness can set you back weeks or even months. Repeated weakness can quickly set you back years!

Millions of parents struggle with temper tantrum teenagers. That's because they were weak and they never gained a reputation for standing firm - and then their spoilt children took advantage of them. And they may carry on taking advantage of them, even when they are grown-up - basically still throwing tantrums and causing trouble to blackmail their parents into giving in to them.

Even with good discipline, however, young children, even well-behaved ones, can be a real handful and it can be exhausting to look after them. But there are many measures you can take to make life easier for yourself. And one of the main things you can do when your kids are very young, is to have a practical house.

You really want an area in the house where you can let your your small children play, without fear of them hurting themselves or breaking things.

Put your ornaments away - and for a few years whilst you have toddlers, arrange your house around your sanity and the safety of your children.

There are plastic inserts you can get for power sockets. There are little rubber devices you can get to cover the sharp corners of tables and shelves. You can have safety catches put on your cupboards.

And perhaps most importantly of all - a mother's best friend; the stairgate! And stairgates can be used, not just on the stairs, but in various doorways around the house. Play pens are useful, of course, but you don't necessarily want to keep your child cooped up in one of them for too long at a time.

Practical flooring also really helps - especially in

the rooms where your child normally plays. When you have a child vomiting, dribbling or in any other way leaking around the house, wipe-clean floors are a godsend. It is so much better to have a practical laminate, tiled or lino floor than to be hopelessly trying to keep your carpets clean.

Later on, as the children grow up, you can change things back if you like - but, for now, peace of mind, your child's safety and making life easier are the priorities. Foregoing practicality to pursue your designer house ideals is really just asking for trouble.

Another important thing to mention at this stage, is potty training.

Modern nappies (diapers) are extremely convenient and they rarely leak. They are also, apparently, very comfortable - even when soiled, it seems. These are good features, of course, but they can also cause a problem when it comes to potty-training. Toddlers are just far too happy to carry on using their nappies.

There are pull-up 'training' nappies that can be used - but by eliminating the mess, they may just prolong the potty training process.

So, really, the solution is just to take the nappies away during the daytime and let your toddler walk freely around, with the potty always on hand. There will likely be some accidents and some mess, but that's what encourages them to use the potty - and that's also one of the reasons why you've put in practical, wipe-clean flooring!

Food

By now, we all ought to know what we should be eating: Very little processed food and lots and lots of wonderfully healthy vegetables - preferably steamed vegetables. But then some parents might ask, "Ah, but what if my child won't eat their vegetables?"

My answer to that would be that in all my years of experience, I've never met a child who wouldn't eat their vegetables.

On the other hand, I have met many parents who start out being anxious that their child won't eat vegetables - and who then pass their own anxieties on to that child. I've met many parents who are too weak-willed to insist their children eat their vegetables. And I've met many parents who don't want to eat many vegetables themselves and can't be bothered to cook vegetables 'just for the children' - and who then make up excuses, falsely claiming that their children 'won't eat their vegetables.' I've known children who are so used to living almost exclusively on junk food, that they are reluctant to eat anything else.

But I have never met a child who genuinely wouldn't eat their vegetables, provided that it was very clearly explained to them that they were not being given a choice in the matter.

You can move babies on to 'whizzed-up' vegetables and potato as soon as you wean them - and then they'll be hooked on the taste and they'll never remember a time when they didn't eat vegetables pretty much every day.

The idea that children don't like vegetables is utter nonsense. Nearly all children absolutely love vegetables - unless they are conditioned not to. And you mustn't let that happen!

Don't like vegetables? I don't have any of that. I simply do not stand for it. I tell children; 'I don't care what you like or don't like. That is your dinner and you will eat it.'

Some children may resist - but never for long, so long as you are strict with them. They're just a bit short-sighted sometimes - but they know when they can't win.

Equally, they soon suss it out if you are weak and pathetic and won't stand up to them. An instinct for sniffing out weakness is something that almost every child is simply born with.

As a parent, it is your job to enable and encourage your children to develop as people who eat healthily and who love eating healthily. You should have no truck with fussy eaters - especially fussy eaters who resist eating their vegetables.

It is a parent's job to decide what food their children should eat. Of course they may be given treats, but only in moderation. And their diet, as a whole, needs to be healthy. It is the duty of every parent to make sure this is the case - provided they are in a position to be able to do so!

Sadly, millions of parents allow their children to gorge on appallingly unhealthy food, and often completely fail to insist that they eat the things that are genuinely good for them. Often, they have kids who throw tantrums if anyone tries to make them eat their vegetables or if they don't get the chips and ice-cream that they demand.

And yet the task in hand could hardly be simpler. As a parent, you simply need to impress upon children some simple rules: You (the parents) decide what they eat and they are to eat it without argument and without exception. They are not to take food without permission and they must eat every last scrap of what you give them. The only exception would be if they are genuinely unwell. How could it be any easier than that?

The reason some kids make a fuss over their food is that they believe they will get their own way if they do. Probably most kids try it at least once - refusing to eat the food they are given - but they will soon stop, so long as parents obey one simple rule: Never give in to them!

If a child says, "But I don't like it!" your duty as a parent is simple: You say, "Nobody asked whether you like it or not. I decide what you eat. That is your food and you will eat every last mouthful." And then, you must insist that that is precisely what they do.

Do not give in to them - however much fuss they make. If you give in once, you create a rod for your own back. They sit there, they eat the food and they do nothing else until it is eaten. If it takes all night, so be it!

If you stand absolutely firm the first time, there may well will never be a second time. Children are very adaptable. If making a fuss clearly isn't going to get them anywhere, they won't do it anymore.

It is a simple question of willpower. It is not in the interests of your child to eat unhealthily. A child can be wilful - but if you, as a parent, do not have the willpower to insist that they eat healthily, then you are not fit to be a parent.

There may sometimes be the problem of overcoming the fear of the unfamiliar. You sometimes get children who claim they don't like something, when what's really happened is that they've never actually properly tried it. And perhaps it isn't like the food they usually eat.

This fear of the unfamiliar may be a reasonably natural fear, but it is made much worse by parents who say things like, "Well, try a little bit and see if you like it." Please don't say anything like that! It is comments like that that may be making your child anxious in the first place. If you act as if there can be no good reason why there should be any problem, your child is far less likely to develop their own anxieties.

On rare occasions, there may be a particular food that a child has genuine problems with. For example, some people are excessively sensitive to curry flavours - and what, for you, seems like a mild curry, seems to them like agony on a plate. Additionally, some food smells can genuinely set off a person's gag reflex, but these are very rare exceptions to the norm and it should not be too difficult to distinguish between a fussy child and a child who is not normally a fussy eater in any way, but who has a genuine problem with one or two specific types of perhaps rather strongly-flavoured foods.

Children who are not made to eat healthily are only likely to have even bigger food-related problems when they are adults. Obesity and other major health problems may result - so it is vitally important to set them off on the right path when they are young.

And as children get older, you must teach them a little about nutrition - about the foods that are especially good for them and the foods that should be avoided, except as a special treat.

And at some stage before they leave home, it really is extremely important that you teach them how to prepare food and cook for themselves. And don't be sexist. Teach the boys as well as the girls. In the modern world, so many men and women leave it until their thirties or even later before they settle down and have families of their own. Thus, even if they do eventually marry a superb cook, they'll have a lot of years as a singleton, in which they'll have to cook for themselves. And when/if they do eventually find a partner, there will be a very good chance that they're not much of a cook anyway. So, it is very important that none of your children leave home without being able to cook a decent range of healthy meals for themselves.

Spoilt

In the old days, it was a common concern, often talked about, that children might become 'spoilt' if they had too many presents and other treats, or if they became too used to having an easy time of things.

These days, it seems, that sort of thing is rarely said and rarely considered. This, however, is a big mistake. It is very much possible to spoil a child - and great care should be taken to avoid causing such terrible harm. A spoilt child is all too likely to become a spoilt adult - leading to all sorts of ongoing problems and all sorts of ongoing misery.

There are some children who are naturally considerate and grateful and who are in very little danger of becoming spoilt, even with rather lax parenting. There are many others, however, who do need to be reminded, reasonably frequently, just how lucky they are - and who are in considerable danger of becoming spoilt, unless great care is taken to keep their feet on the ground.

Thankfully, this does not mean that you cannot treat a child, or, indeed, that you cannot provide for them a luxurious lifestyle, because it isn't actually the gifts and toys and treats that spoil a child - it's bad parenting, pure and simple!

You can 'spoil' children in terms of getting them lots of gifts, holidays, games and giving them a great childhood, but it won't 'spoil' them in a bad way, so long as you withdraw those privileges when they behave badly and do not restore those privileges until the message is clearly understood.

Children who get gifts and treats should be grateful for those gifts and treats - and those gifts and treats should come with firm conditions attached. You can unconditionally love your child, but there should be no unconditional presents, treats or other such privileges.

There are some simple rules that any parent should be clear to their children about: "Treats are only for good children," you should tell them. "Nice toys are only for good children. Computer games are only for good children."

And you should remind children as often as is necessary; "It is Mummy's job and Daddy's job to take nice things away from children who do not behave themselves." Nice things are for good children and not for naughty children. It is a simple as that.

Giving children gifts does not, in itself, spoil them. But giving and letting them keep gifts even when they are badly behaved; that gives the wrong message and teaches the wrong lesson - and that's what spoils them!

Time

All parents get faced with major strategic decisions about how they will bring up their children - and one of the most important of these is about the issue of time.

Parents often wrestle with the trade-off between spending time with children, and being able to provide for them in other ways - especially in terms of buying them things and paying for them to take part in activities or go on trips and holidays.

And, let's be frank; an awful lot of parents get this major strategic decision seriously wrong. Perhaps because of the pressures of our overly commercial, consumerist society, they place far too much emphasis on what they can buy for their children, and far too little emphasis on the importance of spending time with them and being able to do things together as a family.

Sometimes, quite a bit is made of the need to spend time with very young children - but, once they're in school, it's treated as a very different situation. It is as if, by that stage, it's OK to let them go largely unsupported - as if they'll be better off with mates than parents. But, back in reality, they still need parenting - and lots of it. In many practical ways, you can do just as much, if not more for them, when they're in double figures, than when they're younger than that.

Nurseries and schools - these do not and cannot take over the job of parenting for you. They do a different job - and, in very many cases, unfortunately, they don't even do that very well.

Parenting can be a demanding task and it is well to set aside plenty of time to make a good job of it - whatever the age of the child. Unfortunately, the pressures of the modern world can make parents tired and stressed - and keeping your child quiet by buying them things can often seem like the easier option.

Another part of the problem is that a lot of parents don't really especially enjoy spending time with their children. They don't really want to play board games and card games with their children. They don't want to kick a ball around with them. They don't really want to go camping with them. They would see such activities as chores to be avoided, not pleasures to be enjoyed.

They may say they don't do such things with their children merely because they do not have the time. Often, however, their lack of time and energy is largely due to the consequences of their own decisions. It is largely by design - albeit a design they will not admit to. They arrange their lives so that they don't have much time to spend with their children - then try to blame that situation on others, as if they had nothing to do with it.

"We both have to work to be able to pay the mortgage!" they may claim. Well, that may be so - but who made the decision to buy such an unnecessarily expensive house in the first place?

But really, if you don't like spending time with children, then you probably shouldn't be having children in the first place!

It is an appalling truth that a very large proportion of parents never really bother to get to know their children as individual personalities. Conversations - such that there are - focus on such topics as, "What did you *do* today?" Rarely do they ever delve any deeper into the child's thoughts, opinions and ideas.

That, however, is not really good enough. Parents should engage their children in genuinely meaningful conversation - and encourage them to develop and defend their own unique opinions and outlook on life. If, as a parent, you're not really doing that, then you're not doing your job.

Education

Almost all children either begin life with an extensive sense of inquisitiveness or they quickly develop such inquisitiveness. In most cases, however, by the time they leave school, most of this natural inquisitiveness has been eroded away. As to the culprit of this catastrophe, the suspicion must fall on what we curiously still refer to as our education system.

Very often, by the time young people leave school, the wonder of learning has been almost entirely driven from them in favour of indoctrinating them to believe that the point of education is to enable them to pass exams. They learn just what they have to learn in order to get their certificates and secure a job or a place at university. Often, they come to resent having to learn anything at all.

My experience of the problem comes from a UK perspective, but the situation in many other countries appears to be little better - and sometimes even worse. Our education systems are a disaster. Each year, they churn out young people who have been successfully conditioned to be willing to work hard, only so that they can serve as consumers to drive the consumption-based economy, but who are atrociously ill-equipped to make a positive contribution to our society or to the advancement of our culture - or even simply to make good parents themselves.

This is where we come to another of the most important strategic decisions you may have to make as a parent.

Schools work hard to churn out money-obsessed, drinking-obsessed, fashion-obsessed, mobile-phone-obsessed, social-networking and YouTube-obsessed conformists. If you don't want your darling children to end up like that, then you've got some serious parenting to do to counteract the malign influences that commonly infect them in schools.

And in many cases, by far the most effective solution to this problem is not to send your children to school in the first place. Provided you are in a country that hasn't made it illegal to homeschool, then homeschooling is an option that offers enormous potential advantages over sending your children to school.

Unless you are lucky enough to be able to send your children to an exceptionally good school, it is likely to be far easier and more effective to homeschool your children, than to attempt to counteract the ill-effects their school will have on them and on their attitudes towards learning. Why work hard to counteract such harm, when you can simply act to prevent the harm in the first place? Homeschooling really is something that every responsible parent should consider very seriously.

Homeschooling isn't a practical solution for everyone, of course - but if this applies to you, then it is vital that you don't assume that your child will get a good education from their school. This applies regardless of how good the school's reputation may be. I've known plenty of schools with good reputations who still do an appalling job of educating the children in their charge.

On no account should you ever trust a school to oversee the education of your child. That is a job for you - the child's parents. It is certainly not good enough just to assume the school will do anything like a good job of educating your child. In all probability, they'll do an appalling job if you just leave them to it.

Most teachers will want your child to get good grades, because that makes them look good, but they're probably too busy to worry very much about actually educating your child in any broader sense of the word. There are some wonderful teachers, of course, but even many of the best will find it a struggle to put their students' education above the many other demands that are placed on them by the mismanaged 'tick-box' school system in which they work.

In all probability, your child's school is limiting their horizons, not broadening them. And instead of reinforcing good disciplinary standards, they usually undermine them.

Most modern schools are factories of conformism. Our education system is - and I'm not exaggerating about this - largely a system of indoctrination, designed to produce willing workers and willing consumers. That is a tragedy of epic proportions. And protecting your children from the influence and effects of this social indoctrination, is one of your most important jobs as a parent.

But how do you even attempt to perform this task?

Well, your central strategy should be to talk with your child - lots. Don't just politely ask them how their day at school has been. Don't just accept, "Fine," or, "OK, I guess!" for an answer. Set time aside to really talk with them about what they've learnt, about their teachers, about their friends - and be on hand to frequently point out alternative views and perspectives to the ones they're presented with at school.

Encourage your child to always question what they are told - because the last thing you can rely on is for the school to do this vital task for you. Schools are too busy training children to be conformists, who will give only the answers the exam boards deem to be relevant and correct. To them, inquisitive children who question the official line, are basically just trouble-makers. Your task, however, is to save your child from the terrible fate of becoming a zombie-like conformist themselves.

Special Needs

And while we're on the subject of education, it seems like a good moment to mention 'special needs' and 'learning difficulties.'

We hear so much about 'Attention-Deficit-Hyperactivity-Disorder' (ADHD) and other trendy, alleged conditions. Far too much, I think! Indeed, we continue to be in the midst of an obsession with special needs.

Now, not for a minute would I deny that some children have real problems and real learning difficulties. But today, unfortunately, there is an industry of excuse generation that is quick to label children as having special needs or learning difficulties or 'conditions' such as ADHD (or whatever term is currently fashionable).

In many cases, I suspect, it isn't a genuine problem with the child - the problems are just a symptom of inadequate parenting and an inadequate education system.

Of course, parents don't like to be told that their child is simply a brat and that the appalling behaviour of their child is due to their woeful lack of basic parenting skills. They much prefer to hear that their child has a 'condition' - so they can blame their child's problems on the condition, rather than accepting the responsibility for their own failings as parents.

Please, if your child is badly behaved and causing problems, if they are failing to pay attention, if they are not learning as quickly as they ought to be, don't be quick or overly eager to allow your child to be labelled as having special needs. Look first and foremost to improve your parenting skills.

After all, no-one is perfect - so before accepting the labels that the machinery of politically-correct excuse generation is all too eager to attach to your child, have a good think about whether you, as their parents, are doing your job properly.

There is no good reason to be defensive over your parenting skills. It is practically impossible to bring up children without making mistakes. The important thing is always to be trying to improve.

And as well as looking at your own parenting, take a good look at the behaviour of your child's school or nursery. Are they doing their job properly? Are they providing an environment in which children can properly concentrate? Are they implementing a proper disciplinary system?

In the old days, if a child couldn't spell very well, we just gave them more frequent spelling tests. 'But what if they are dyslexic?' you may ask.

Well, if a child is not dyslexic, but they can't spell very well, the remedy is; more reading, more writing, more spelling practice and more spelling tests.

And if a child is dyslexic and can't spell very well, do you know what the main remedy in that situation is? The main solution, in that situation is, in fact; more reading, more writing, more spelling practice and more spelling tests.

If a child is badly behaved, what is the solution? The solution is to apply a rigorous disciplinary system and firm punishments, so that the child quickly realises that bad behaviour doesn't pay.

But if a badly-behaved child has ADHD, what is the solution then? The solution is to apply a rigorous disciplinary system and firm punishments, so that the child quickly realises that bad behaviour doesn't pay.

So, if the solution is the same, what is the point of labelling a child as dyslexic or as having ADHD?

Unfortunately, what often happens in real life, is

that labels are used as excuses - not as excuses for action, but as excuses for inaction and for accepting lower standards from the child in question.

Now, there are, of course, genuine, extreme cases in which children really do have exceptional difficulties of one kind or another and may benefit from specialist help.

In many cases, however, 'dyslexic' children are essentially just children who need to work harder than others to improve their spelling and their reading and writing capabilities. And children with ADHD are just naughty children who need some firm disciplinary measures to be applied.

Playtime

Whether it's playing sports, board games, card games or computer games or just messing around with toys, sand, water or sticks - it's all good.

Whether it's a small child just casually brumming their toy cars around the floor or an older child playing table tennis or chess, I'm just a huge fan of allowing children of all ages to have loads and loads of time for fun, games, sports and just playing around.

It seems to me that playtime is incredibly important to any child's happiness and well-being. Playtime is fantastic. The trouble is that millions of children don't get anywhere near enough of it.

For many children, a typical school day might involve about 7 hours of being at school, perhaps an hour or so of travelling to and from school, an hour or two more of homework time, alongside time for eating and washing, leaving only an hour or two, or perhaps much less, for playing and having fun.

That's not what we should be aiming for at all! Instead of nine hours for schooling and two hours for play, I would have it the other way around: two hours of schooling and nine hours of playtime.

'But what about the child's education?' some may ask.

'Exactly!' I would reply. Play isn't just fun. Playtime is the best education system we've ever encountered. It's nature's education system. It's the very best way of all to learn and develop and expand your interests and your capabilities - and it always has been!

Informal play is particularly important to young children, but more formal, structured activities become more important as children get older.

I may be a rather wizened old nanny and I may be a fairly strict disciplinarian, but when it comes to bringing up children, there must be few people more appreciative of the value of games.

From simple children's card games to board games such as Monopoly and advanced strategy games, such as chess and poker, there is a vast range of skills to be learnt and developed; from the simple ability to understand and follow rules, to mathematical skills, judgement skills, negotiating skills and the ability to develop advanced tactics and strategies to outmanoeuvre your opponents.

Did you hear me right? Did I mention poker? Yes, I certainly did! Playing poker really is an excellent learning experience for all children. I've given poker lessons to pretty much all my charges and every one of them has benefited from them very considerably.

I'm not much of a chess player, but I'm good enough to whip the bottom of any little scallywag who doesn't bother concentrating!

I'm a particular fan of the educational value of board games. Board games have rules to follow - not rules that are automatically enforced by a computer, but rules you have to keep an eye on yourself.

It is a character-building challenge to be innovative and to come up with winning strategies, and to do so fairly, within the rules of the game, with good sportsmanship. So many life lessons can be gleaned from playing board games.

And then there are sports! And what could be healthier and more character-building than taking part in a wide range of sports?

It's playtime that makes children happy. Let them play and play and play. Children should have lots and lots of playtime, pretty much every day.

It can, of course, be difficult to fit much playtime around school and homework - which is one of the top reasons why bringing up happy and contented children may be so much easier if you are able to educate them at home. Unfortunately, not everyone is able to do that.

But if it is at all in your power to do so, please try to ensure that when your kids grow up, they can never, in all reasonableness, claim that they didn't have enough time to play when they were kids.

Healthy, thoughtful, hard-working and happy adults are most likely to develop from children who had plenty of time to play.

Finally, on this subject; here's a little question a lot of parents seem to struggle with: When you're playing all those healthy sports and brain-stimulating games with your kids, should you let them win? To which my answer would be, 'No - not unless you're doing it as a joke!'

Some people seem to believe that it will make children depressed or insecure if you don't let them win - but that's mainly just paranoid nonsense.

Besides which, it's undermining the educational value of the games and sports you play. Dad *should* be beating you at chess, because he's studied the game a lot longer than you have. Mum *should* be beating you at tennis, because she's spent a lot more time developing her shots and improving her hand-eye coordination than you have. You're not supposed to win straight away! You can win when you've put in lots of effort and become good enough to win.

There's no call to lie to your children and risk giving them a false sense of reality - perhaps distorting their perception of the value of hard work, thoughtfulness, determination and perseverance.

It's not losing that makes kids feel insecure. They became insecure when they can't trust what you say. They get insecure when you fuss over them, fretfully 'protecting' them from feelings of inadequacy - all the time making matters worse.

Have confidence that they won't fall to pieces when they lose a game, or if people laugh when they get something wrong, or if someone criticises them. Bring them up to believe this is all perfectly normal and nothing to be concerned about.

If you want to have a close, competitive game, just have a handicap system. Play chess minus your queen. Take on three kids at once at football. Give a head start in a running race. But don't lie and cheat your way to making your kids feel artificially good about themselves. In the long run, it's counterproductive.

It's if you mollycoddle them that they might then have a problem and start crying when they are eventually allowed to lose at something.

They should lose at sports and games until they put the work in to get good enough to win. Then they'll have good reason to be proud of themselves.

Friends

It's tough, perhaps especially as a child, to have worries about fitting in. Fortunately, I have a very simple solution.

My solution isn't that you should help your children find ways to fit in with their 'friends.' My solution is to teach them that they shouldn't even try.

You should want your children to be resistant to peer group pressure. There's all sorts of unhappiness waiting for anyone who isn't. So, you should always advise them that being popular and 'fitting in' are of little importance.

'Just concentrate on being good, decent and kind,' you should tell them. 'If you're good, decent and kind and people still don't want to be friends with you, then they're idiots and not the sorts of people you would want to have as friends anyway!'

Problem solved!

Screens

We hear complaints sometimes, that kids spend far too much time 'on screens' - watching TV, playing computer games and surfing the internet for social media updates and YouTube videos. I'm old-fashioned in a lot of ways, so you might perhaps expect me to take a dim view of screen time.

I don't, however, see computer games or TV or web-surfing as inherently bad. They are marvellous inventions if used wisely. Many children have great fun engaging in such activities - and some computer games and YouTube videos are actually very educational. In fact, I would say that services such as YouTube offer a far superior opportunity for education, than do the vast majority of traditional TV channels.

Real problems mainly arise when children spend too much time with low-quality, brainless games, brainless films, brainless TV shows and and brainless YouTube videos that aren't educational and don't challenge them in any meaningful way.

And further problems arise when screen time displaces healthier activities that many children aren't getting enough of in any case - playing outside, enjoying the sunshine, enjoying nature, playing sports, having conversations, reading books etc.

But if children are well-behaved and do get plenty of exercise and spend a decent amount of time outside and do their schooling and play with their friends and have conversations and play sports and board games and card games and read books, then I don't see any convincing reason why we should be stingy about allowing them to have the screen time that they clearly enjoy.

There are all sorts of things for children to learn and skills for them to develop through watching TV and playing computer games. Just be sure to guide them towards stimulating, thinking-based games - and stimulating, thought-provoking, high-quality TV, movies and videos, not brainless reality shows.

And I wouldn't worry too much about children playing violent video games or watching violent films. So long as children get out and about and have plenty of experience of the real world, they can perfectly well understand that real life is not a video game - and that violent behaviour can be fun in video games, but should be kept out of real life as much as possible.

Some people claim that violent games and films make people violent in real life. In fact, I don't think there is any convincing scientific evidence of this. If anything, violent games and films help people to relax and give them a chance to work out their frustrations - perhaps even preventing some of the violence that might otherwise occur in the real world.

I've actually taken part in a 'frag-fest' myself (difficult as that may be to imagine!) - and I must say I really rather enjoyed myself. And afterwards, I had absolutely no heightened urge whatsoever to kill anyone in real life!

The problem is not violence or 'inappropriate content.' The problems come from games that fail to properly stimulate children to use and exercise their minds. Mindless shooting games can be fun and can be a stress-reliever, but they are for short bursts of fun, not for long hours of play.

But there is a screen-related problem that really is harming children - and that is their obsession with their phones and with social media sites.

These are the obsessions that prompt them to be constantly anxious about what other people are doing and saying. They are constantly fearful of missing out on some sort of 'vital' social interaction, should they turn their phones off for even a few minutes.

And they become addicted to obsessing about the superficial attention gauges of messages and likes and upvotes for the banal, attention-seeking posts, tweets and selfies that they are constantly encouraged to produce.

I am of the opinion that some nice quiet time spent alone with a computer game is probably much healthier than the constant, but largely mindless social interaction most children and most adults seem to be embroiled in these days.

The constant need for approval, or even just acknowledgement, seems to be the most worrying - and likely very harmful - aspect of these obsessions.

So, is it harming your child that they are obsessed with their phone and with social media? Yes. Yes it is.

So, if you allow your child to have a smartphone, you should also make sure they practise going without it - for example, they can go on camping trips and leave their mobile behind.

If they are not at ease with being without their phone for a few hours each day or for a few days whilst they are on holiday, then they are in the grip of a worrying obsession - and should probably have their phone taken away for a while, so they can become used to not having it and learn to be less reliant on it.

Their phone obsession may be training them to need almost constant feedback from other people - to validate their looks, their decisions, their general behaviour and even their very existence. That's a very unhealthy, stress-inducing and potentially dangerous obsession to suffer from - and a habit that may urgently need to be broken.

Camping

Just a quick note to say: Don't underestimate the enormous benefit to be derived from going on camping trips. Proper camping, I mean - not 'RV camping'!

Fresh air, exercise, map-reading, camp cooking, campcraft, self-reliance, getting away from computers and phones for a while - can there be anything more wholesome?

I still take kids camping, even at my age and despite my sore hip and dodgy knees. It's one of the very best things you can do for them!

Money

Most adults, it seems, are pretty terrible with money. They make terrible spending decisions and make themselves poor by wasting their money, not just on things that are unnecessary, but often on things that do them no good at all or which are actually bad for them.

But it's your job, as a parent, to try to prepare your children for when they'll be in charge of their own money and have to make important financial decisions for themselves.

You want them to be financially smart enough that they won't fritter away their money on unhealthy takeaways, ridiculously expensive smartphones or holidays where they drink too much, eat too much and spend too much time in the sun, seemingly trying to get skin cancer.

But how do you go about preparing your children to be financially astute and sensible adults?

Well, you can, if you like, give children an allowance each week or month, as they get older - so that they can have practice in managing their own finances. You can give them lessons about credit cards and compound interest rates.

There are two things, however, that I consider much more important.

Firstly, you ought to be setting your children a good example. How can you reasonably expect your children to learn to manage money intelligently, if you've been setting a bad example all their lives, by wasting money yourself?

And be especially careful to be money-wise when it comes to buying things for your children. Fortunately, there are plenty of ways to keep them entertained, without spending a fortune - so when they want the latest toys or gadgets, available at extortionate prices, say no to them. Say no to your kids - and they'll be better able to say no to themselves when they are adults.

You can buy all sorts of wonderful things for your children, but tell them very firmly; "I'm not paying rip-off prices!"

For example; never buy your child the latest games console and the latest games at premium prices. If they are lucky enough to have a games console, get them an older console and some second hand games.

Better still; get them an old PC, perhaps from ebay. You can get some excellent games for those that are a small fraction of the price of the up-to-date console games, but which are much longer-lasting and many times more educational. I know several young lads who often rave about the classic PC games they have in their collections - and having seen some of them, I think they're entirely right to do so. Put it like this: If you enjoyed playing computer games when you were a child, there's no good reason why your children couldn't enjoy exactly the same games you enjoyed.

Indeed, there's rarely any good reason to splurge on getting your kids the latest, most-premium-priced version of anything. Don't play along with the greedy marketing departments of the world's money-hungry corporations, who try to brainwash children into demanding their products. By all means, buy a company's products if they offer you a good deal - but not otherwise!

And, secondly, you should be encouraging your children to have a healthy attitude towards money and the value of money - as well as a healthy scepticism towards the overly consumerist attitudes so common in our modern societies.

Encourage them to observe the celebrities and

other rich people who, despite all their wealth, seem to live the most dreadfully unhappy lives - lurching from one failed relationship to another.

Encourage them to notice the many silly people around who repeatedly seek attention, not by actually doing anything worthwhile, but by buying things in the desperate hope that other people may be jealous of them as a result. They spend a fortune on the latest iPhone, not because they need a new phone, but because they get a momentary thrill from the thought that other people might look at them and say 'Oooo - have you seen that? She's got the new iPhone!'

Encourage them to observe the silly people who try to buy other people's affections - and how that strategy almost always ends up in failure.

Encourage them to take note of the people who slave away for long hours each week at work, so that they can have an expensive house with a lovely garden, that they never get time to sit in and enjoy.

Point out the silly people who work hard to earn extra money, only to waste that extra income on more expensive versions of things they already have - like a pointlessly expensive sports car that, just as pointlessly, can apparently go twice as fast as the speed limit - and which is no better at getting them to work than the far cheaper, more fuel-efficient car they just got rid of.

Through simple observation and discussion, children can learn that money is not the simple ticket to success that our society often assumes it to be - and you should encourage your children to make those observations and take part in those discussions.

Sex, Alcohol, Drugs and Gambling

In due course, your little darlings are going to be going out into an adult world and dealing with adult problems - such as those related to alcohol, drugs, sex and gambling.

Naturally, we try to shield children from these concerns when they are young, but we also have the responsibility of preparing them to deal with these issues when they are adults - and often, unfortunately, before they are adults.

And a major dilemma parents face is when to tell children about these things and how much to tell them. Naturally, we want to preserve our children's childhoods. We don't want them to be overly concerned with such issues when they are young. However; if in doubt, they need to know. The worst mistake is to leave it too late.

I know! These are concerns you want to keep your precious darling away from, but before too long, they will be adults in an adult world and they will have to deal with these things themselves - and your job is to prepare them so that they deal with them well.

It may be an awkward duty to fulfil, but someone has to tell children about sex, drugs and gambling - and it's the parents who should be doing that job. Do not leave it to their school or to their peers - either of which would probably do a terrible job of it.

Another dilemma parents face is in regard to *how* they should approach these issues and what sort of advice to give.

A common concern is that if you take an overly conservative, puritanical approach and say, basically; never drink alcohol, never smoke, never take drugs, never gamble and never have sex outside marriage, you will be considered such a ridiculously old-fashioned, overly-protective fuddy-duddy, that your growing children will basically just ignore you. And, unfortunately, this concern often then leads to parents taking a ridiculously permissive approach.

The modern, politically-correct approach is basically one, not of saying to children that they should not have underage sex, but of saying that, if they do, please use a condom. And that, frankly, is taking things ridiculously - and often very harmfully - too far.

If your children don't trust you when you warn against getting drunk, taking drugs or having underage sex, then the problem isn't that you are giving them bad advice. The problem is that your children don't trust your good advice. And if they don't trust your advice, the root of the problem may well be that you simply haven't been honest with them and/or that you have often given them a lot of rather biased, unscientific advice over the years. Be honest with your children from the start and then perhaps you won't have this problem in the first place.

It's true that you can go too far with a puritanical approach too, but that's not usually the problem we have nowadays. The problem today is political-correctness essentially encouraging children to do all the things we don't want them to do.

Alcohol, drugs and underage sex are potentially very damaging indeed - and parents should never be afraid to tell it like it is.

Try to give principled and evidence-based, not prejudice-based advice on all matters, at all times. And, above all, be honest with your children - so that they come to realise that the advice you give them is generally sound, helpful and well worth listening to.

In warning children of dangers, don't exaggerate, but do tell it how it is. You don't want your children to become alcoholics, but an occasional drink probably won't do them any harm, so don't claim that it will. Tell them honestly about the harm caused by smoking. Don't be hysterical, but do show them the pictures of smoking-damaged lungs.

Do make sure your children know about sexually-transmitted diseases and don't be afraid to say that abstinence is indeed the best way to avoid them. Prepare them also for the social forces that might push them towards sex before they are ready.

Gambling is a rather different problem from drugs and underage sex, because children can become involved in perfectly harmless 'gambling' activities whilst they are still quite young. Many children enjoy an occasional trip to a 'penny arcade.' And when they're adults, they might enjoy an occasional punt on a horse or an evening out at a casino.

Naturally, we wouldn't want our children, when they grow up, to develop costly gambling habits or become problem gamblers. Out of fear of this happening, some parents bar their children from all gambling activities, no matter how trivial the stakes involved. I suggest, however, that this is probably entirely the wrong approach.

Completely shielding your children from all gambling opportunities is not going to provide them with the understanding of possible temptations and pitfalls of gambling excessively.

The better solution, I suggest, is for them to feel the gambling buzz whilst under your careful supervision. Have a friendly little bet on their behalf on a horse race. Play some gambling-style card games. Let them play at the penny arcade occasionally.

Give them a chance to understand and experience that these are fun activities that will, nevertheless, lose them money. Disabuse them of the idea that there is money to be made from gambling on horses or at the casino. Teach them about how the odds are fixed in the bookmaker's or casino's favour. Let them experience the gambling buzz and learn to resist it - all whilst under your watchful supervision.

Don't, whatever you do, attempt to shield them from all gambling activities until they are adults, and then suddenly expect them to be able to cope maturely with the lures and dangers of gambling.

If you child grows up to have a gambling problem, I suggest it almost certainly won't be because they were introduced to gambling as a child. The problem is far more likely to be that you failed to introduce them to gambling and failed to teach them the risks and temptations of gambling when they were safely under your supervision.

Tell your children about sex, in plenty of time, and tell them not to have it until they are adults - and preferably only when they are in a settled relationship.

Don't get into a stupid game of trying to second guess them and thinking that if you tell them not to do it, they will immediately go out and do it. No they won't - not if you have done your job properly as a parent.

And don't, for goodness' sake, brainwash them about how being homosexual is perfectly normal and 'just as valid' as being heterosexual. God or nature has decided that heterosexual relationships are the ones that produce children. In that very

79

important sense, they will always be inherently superior to homosexual relationships.

This does not mean, of course, that you won't always love your child, even if they do end up being gay, but if you are like most parents, you will probably strongly prefer them not to be - and there's no good reason why you should feel obliged to pretend otherwise.

Don't tell your child you'll be perfectly happy if they are gay, if it isn't true. Most parents would be rather upset and disappointed if their child was gay - and that's perfectly natural and OK. And no, it isn't homophobic to feel that way!

Just be honest. If you've brought them up properly, your children will understand perfectly well that you won't always agree with them and you won't always be pleased with their behaviour or their choices.

And for the love of God, do not pander to the politically-correct madness that your child might have been 'born in the wrong body' and might require 'gender reassignment.' There are no transsexual children - only children whose parents are idiots. There are no boys born in female bodies or girls born in male bodies. With the exception of those who genuinely have to struggle with physically-real, intersex medical conditions, it's all a load of politically-correct, utter nonsense! If you were born a boy, you are a boy. If you were born a girl, you are a girl. That's just the way it is. And in my book, 'gender reassignment' for a child is simply child abuse.

A Broken Chain

One of my biggest concerns of all about parenting today, is about how the traditional chain of experience - of parents passing on their knowledge, skills, interests and wisdom to their children - has been severely damaged and, in many instances, almost completely broken.

Today, both parents of a child are often largely disconnected from their child - not just because they often both spend long hours away at work, but because of the widespread cultural assumption that children aren't and wouldn't be interested in what their parents can teach them - and perhaps not interested in anything their parents might say to them. By default, they are then left to be overly-influenced - some might even say 'brainwashed' - by their schools, their peers and the marketing departments of large corporations.

It is a devastatingly damaging change that seems to have taken place in our society over recent decades. Whereas, once, parents used to see it as their duty to teach their children how to cook, how to put up a tent or how to wire a plug, very few parents seem to do that sort of thing anymore. Whereas parents used to teach their kids card games or how to play chess, very few now seem to bother. Whereas many parents used to share their interests and hobbies with their children, most now either don't seem to bother or don't even have much in the way of interests to share anyway - besides watching the TV or going shopping!

But it's not just about missing skills and interests - it's about missing relationships. Whereas families used to come together for meals - and chat together - many now just have their meals in front of the TV. Many don't even have their meals in the same room, preferring instead to take their food off to their own rooms, to eat it in front of their own individual screen, as they check on Facebook, Twitter or Instagram updates or watch mindless YouTube videos. Some kids don't come downstairs to ask when dinner will be ready - they just send a text message down instead!

Many parents are very largely cut off from their children and have very little to do with them, even though they live in the same house.

As a society, we have indulged in what has been a vast and ill-considered experiment - and, quite frankly, a disastrous one. The system that has lasted many thousands of years - of parents passing on their knowledge and experience and interests to their children - has been largely abandoned, in a few short decades, in favour of a largely parent-free alternative that does not work very well.

And amongst those skills that used to get passed down, but often no longer are, are the very skills of parenting that we have been talking about.

A large proportion of today's parents have very limited parenting skills. They couldn't pass on much in the way of parenting skills to their children, because they don't have the skills themselves. And what limited skills they have, often don't get passed on, because their busy lifestyles leave them with little energy and insufficient inclination to make any real effort at doing so.

It's a similar situation to when parents fail to pass on cooking skills. Once the chain of experience is broken - and parents fail to pass on their skills - it becomes an enormous problem that can be extremely difficult to fix. Good habits and valuable skills are lost - and it can be very difficult getting those habits and skills back into the system - back into circulation.

And adding to the problem is that people who do have the necessary skills and experience, are reluctant to help, because of the ridiculous political-correctness that results in people seeing an offer of help as a criticism - or even as an insult.

In many otherwise prosperous countries, we have a crisis of parenting. Many parents spend very little time with their children and have little time, energy or inclination to properly get to know them.

Parents and children live in the same house, yet barely have a clue about what each others' opinions might be on anything other than banal topics, such as who should get ejected next from some inane reality TV show or other!

Millions of parents do very little with their children at all. They don't read with their children. They don't play games together. They don't eat together. They don't even watch films or TV together. They don't really talk in any meaningful way. Other than in superficial ways, they barely share their lives at all.

It's wrong, it's a disaster and it's time for this dreadful experiment to end.

Values

It isn't just skills, knowledge and interests that parents are reluctant to pass on to their children. It's also values.

Parents are reluctant and embarrassed to try to pass on values, as if that might be thought of as brainwashing - but that's no good excuse for not discussing values at all.

As a parent, it's perfectly reasonable to try to pass on your values. There's nothing wrong with that, so long as you also encourage your children to develop the inclination and the skills to question what they are being told, including what you tell them.

If we make no attempt to instil values in children (or, at least, discuss and encourage children to develop them), then what we're really doing is leaving a vacuum that often just gets filled by the shallow, consumerist, populist, PC pressures that are all around us today. And that can be disastrous!

And Finally

It seems to me that we can make the world a far better place if only we can firstly achieve one little thing; become better parents.

It is hard to imagine many problems in the world that could not be helped through better parenting.

I hope this book will help.

And try to enjoy yourselves. Being a good parent is not a burden - it's a privilege.

Further Information

To learn more about Nanny Phillips, please visit:

www.IMOS.org.uk/Nanny

Printed in Great Britain
by Amazon